POTS!
GW01606886

# WHAT THE POTS

BY LM HENRY

AN ILLUSTRATOR'S TOUR OF POSTURAL ORTHOSTATIC TACHYCARDIA SYNDROME

A BOOK TO HELP POTS

ISBN: 979-8-218-29122-8

# AFTERWORD:

Dr. Rob Wilson

I WAS AN ATHLETE, SINGER, STAR GAZER, MUSICIAN, DRIVER, BIKER RIDER, SKATEBOARDER, WORKER, GARDENER, DANCER, AND WRITER BEFORE POTS. I WAS AND STILL BRAVE, FUN, SMART, CREATIVE, ADVENTUROUS, IMPORTANT, LOVED, STRONG, AND PROUD TO BE ME.

HEY, LOOK OUT!!!

CLUNK IT ALL WENT

LOOK UP!, FALLING FROM THE SKY, WHAT ARE THOSE THINGS?

CLUNK!!!!

WHY WAS I SMASHED WITH ALL THOSE POTS OUT OF NOWHERE?

POTS, WHAT IS THAT?

POTS IS A MEDICAL CONDITION KNOWN AS POSTURAL ORTHOSTATIC TACHYCARDIA SYNDROME.

P.O.T.S.

POTS HAPPENS FOR MANY REASONS. IT CAN HAPPEN SUDDENLY AND FOR MANY REASONS. IT JUST FEELS LIKE IT IS COMING FROM OUTER SPACE.

POTS IS DIAGNOSED BY THE CLINICAL STORY AND A TILT TABLE. THE TILT TABLE MEASURES BLOOD PRESSURE AND HEART RATE. THE TEST HELP SHOWS WHAT HAPPENS WHEN YOU ARE HAVING POTS SYMPTOMS. IT MIGHT REMIND YOU OF A SCIENTISTS TEST ON A MONSTER, BUT IT IS A TEST TO HELP YOU.

EVERYONE HAS SOMETHING IN THEIR BODY CALLED ADRENALINE TO HELP AND PROTECT THEM FROM HARM. IN POTS THE SIGNALS DO NOT WORK RIGHT ANYMORE. THIS ADRENALINE CAUSES THE "FIGHT OR FLIGHT" RESPONSE OF SURVIVAL IN THE BODY. THIS ADRENALINE RUSH HELPS IN POTS WHEN THE SIGNALS ARE NOT GETTING THROUGH.

POTS PATIENTS CANNOT REGULATE THEIR BLOOD PRESSURE. THE BLOOD PRESSURE WANTS TO DROP AND AT TIMES CAN SPIKE. IT CAN BE A BLOOD PRESSURE SEESAW.

PEOPLE WITH POTS HAVE HEARTS THAT FEEL LIKE THEY WANT TO DANCE. THEIR HEARTS WILL RACE WITH OFTEN LITTLE ACTIVITY. THE TACHYCARDIA IS THE HIGH AND FAST HEARTBEATS OF POTS.

185!

POTS IS STILL NEUROLOGICAL. CAN CAUSE BRAIN FOG, HEAD PAINS, MIGRAINES, CONFUSION, FORGETFULNESS, AND DIZZINESS. IT CAN FEEL LIKE YOUR NERVOUS SYSTEMS IS A BIG JIGSAW PUZZLE TOSSED AND SCATTTERED WITH YOU TRYING TO JUST CONSTANTLY PUTTING THEM TOGETHER.

L M H

THE BARORECEPTOR ARE THE SIGNALS TO KEEP THE BLOOD FLOWING FROM THE NERVES, HEART, BLOOD VESSELS, AND BRAIN. THE BARORECEPTOR IS PART OF THE POTS GAME.

THE ADRENALINE OF POTS CAN MAKE YOUR GUT AND DIGESTION ACT WEIRD. YOU CAN HAVE NAUSEA, ACID REFLUX, GASTROPARESIS, FEEDING PROBLEMS, SWALLOWING CHALLENGES, AND NUTRITION CHALLENGES. YOU CANNOT REST OR DIGEST IN THE ADRENALINE.

WE HAVE 10 WATER BOTTLES OF BLOOD IN US. ABOUT 2 BOTTLES DROP WHEN WE STAND UP BECAUSE OF GRAVITY. POTS CANNOT REGULATE THE BLOOD FLOW OF THESE BOTTLES MOVING UP AND DOWN. A PERSON WITH POTS CAN FEEL DIZZY, LIGHTHEADED, NEAR FAINTING, FAINT, WEAK, AND WALKING CHALLENGES.

POTS CAN CAUSE WEAK ARMS AND LEGS FEELINGS. THE LEGS CAN FEEL WEAK, HEAVY, WOBBLY, OR LIKE JELLY. EVERYDAY STUFF CAN BE A CHALLENGE OR BATTLE.

FATIGUE IS ONE OF THE MOST COMMON SYMPTOMS OF POTS. ONE CAN FEEL JUST DRAINED OF ALL OF ONE'S ENERGY. YOUR ENERGY MAY NOT BE THERE TO GET THE TASK, JOB, OR SHOW UP FOR THE GAME.

APPLE A DAY KEEPS THE DOCTOR AWAY, BUT YOU A NEED MEDICAL TEAM TO HELP WITH POTS. YOU NEED SOME SOME GOOD APPLES ON YOUR MEDICAL TEAM.

POTS IS A DIFFICULT CONDITION TO LIVE WITH AS WELL TO TREAT AT TIMES. THERE IS MUCH MEDICAL CARE, TESTING, AND DOUBTS TO YOU ARE DIAGNOSED. LOOKING AROUND TO FIND LOVE AND SUPPORT IS IMPORTANT. LOOK OUT THE WINDOW WITH THE STRUGGLES NOW HOPEFULLY SOON THERE YOU MAY FEEL BETTER SOON AND BE PART OF THIS BIG, BEAUTIFUL WORLD.

POTS
LMH

POTS HAS UPS AND DOWNS. POTS HAS SETBACKS. KEEP TRYING AND WITH YOUR MEDICAL TEAM TO RECLAIM YOUR HEALTH AND LIFE AGAIN. DO NOT WORRY ABOUT THE SETBACKS BECAUSE TOMORROW YOU CAN FEEL EVEN BETTER.

POTS
LMH

AFTER BEING DIAGNOSED

I AM,

SPORTSFAN, SINGALONGER, STARGAZER, MUSIC LISTENER, JOYRIDER, EXERCISE BIKERIDER, LOVES TO WEAR SKATE CLOTHES, WORKS FROM HOME, ROOT SOUP COOK, THEATER VIEWER SPECTATOR, AUTHOR, AND ARTIST.

BRAVE, FUN, SMART, CREATIVE, ADVENTUROUS, IMPORTANT, LOVED, STRONG, AND PROUD TO BE ME.

THE BOOK IS DEDICATED TO:

GOD FOR GIVING ME STRENGTH , I NEED IT

TO MY FAMILY WHO I LOVE WITH ALL MY HEART!

TO MY FATHER, DUCK FOR ALWAYS TALKING BASEBALL WITH ME.

TO MY BROTHERS, BILLY AND DANNY, FOR DROPPING EVERYTHING WHENEVER I NEED. YOU ALWAYS MAKE ME LIKE ME.

TO MY MOMMY, WHO DOES EVERYTHING, EVERY TO

MAKE ME FEEL CARED FOR AND LOVED.

TO ALL THE BEAUTIFUL PEOPLE, I HAVE MET ALONG THE WAY WHO HELPED ME AND HAVE SEEN ME AS A PERSON.

TO COFFEE FOR HELPING ME TO GET THIS BOOK DONE. EVEN IF IT WAS DECAF MOST OF THE TIME

I HAVE POTS AND YOU P.A.N.S. ( PLENTY 'A' NOGGIN SCRATCHIN ), THAT IS BRAVERY.

# AFTERWARD:

BEING A PHYSICIAN IS A PRIVILEGE. A PERSON ENTERS A ROOM OR YOU ENTER THAT PERSON'S SPACE WHEN YOU ARE THE PHYSICIAN. AS A PHYSICIAN THERE IS AN IMMEDIATE GIVEN OF TRUST THAT SOMEONE WILL SHARE ONE'S STORY. THE STORY THAT SOMETHING IS WRONG AND DIFFERENT THAN BEFORE IN ONESELF. THIS IS ONE OF THE MANY HONORS OF THIS WORK. WHAT IS NOT SPOKEN IS THE JOURNEY OF TRAVELING WITH THE PATIENT OR THE PERSON WHO IS THE PATIENT. TRAVEL WITH THE PATIENT IN ALL THE GOOD, NOT SO GOOD, AND BAD OF BEING SICK. YOU HAVE THE OPPORTUNITY TO LEARN FROM EACH PATIENT ABOUT MEDICINE AND JUST LIFE. LINNY ENTERED MY LIFE ABOUT A DECADE AGO. SHE HAS TAUGHT ME SO MUCH. SHE IS JOY, IMPORTANT INSIGHTS, DECENCY, ART, AND HOPES. SHE SEES THE WORLD IN WAYS THAT IS NEEDED. I AM GRATITUDE FOR HER.

HER PHYSICIAN,

DR. ROB WILSON

Printed in Great Britain
by Amazon